The Three Sisters

Beans

Corn

Squash

by Laura Cerier
illustrated by David Austin Clar

![Houghton Mifflin logo] HOUGHTON MIFFLIN   BOSTON

Printed in China

ISBN-13: 978-0-547-02861-3
ISBN-10: 0-547-02861-X

5 6 7 8 9 0940 15 14 13 12
4500351683

Let's plant a garden!

First you will need supplies.

You need shovels, seeds, and a hose.

You can also buy plants.
Some plants have a scent
that keeps bugs away.
You can buy those too!

Next, you need to
get the soil ready for planting.
You will need to dig with
your shovel.
It's hard work digging out
tough roots and rocks.
Use your muscles!

Now it is time to plant your seeds.
What will you plant?
Corn, beans, and squash are
three plants that help
each other grow.
Sometimes they are called the
three sisters.

Corn is a plant that grows tall.
Beans need to climb up
something tall.
So the bean plants climb up the
corn stalks.
Squash plants grow big leaves.
The big leaves make shade.
The shade stops weeds
from growing.

Corn

Beans

Squash

You plant the three sisters in hills.
First, you make a small hill of soil.
Then you push some corn seeds
into the hill.
Next, you plant bean seeds
in a circle around the corn hill.
Then you plant squash seeds
in a circle around the bean circle.

Planting a Three Sisters Garden

Corn

Beans

Squash

At first, your garden might look
plain, but just wait until it starts
to grow!
You will need to water it every day.
Very soon you will see wrinkled
leaves growing.
Then your plants will begin
blooming.
And next vegetables will begin
to grow!

It is fun to pick vegetables from
your own garden.
Soon you will have baskets
full of vegetables.
The three sisters help
each other grow.

The three sisters taste great together, too!

You can make a Three Sisters Stew with your family.

"Do you want a second helping?" they will ask.

You will give a big nod yes!

Three Sisters Stew

2 cups corn
2 cups beans
2 cups butternut squash
5 cups water
2 tablespoons melted
   butter
2 tablespoons flour
pepper, sage, thyme

Responding

Word Builder Many words have words that mean the opposite. Fancy is the opposite of plain. Copy the chart and add more words.

Word	Opposite
plain	fancy
tough	soft
wrinkled	?
big	?

✎ Write About It

Text to Self There are many kinds of gardens. Write a few sentences describing a garden you would like to plant. Would it be vegetables or flowers? Plain or fancy? Use words from the Word Builder.

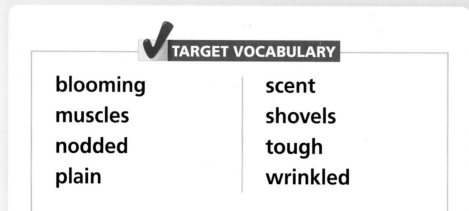

blooming	**scent**
muscles	**shovels**
nodded	**tough**
plain	**wrinkled**

✓ **TARGET STRATEGY** **Analyze/Evaluate** Tell how you feel about the text, and why.

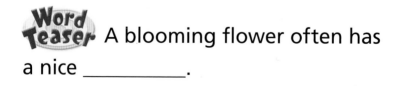 A blooming flower often has a nice _____.